THE MEXICAN-AMERICAN WAR

By SUDIPTA BARDHAN-QUALLEN

BLACKBIRCH PRESS
An imprint of Thomson Gale, a part of The Thomson Corporation

Detroit • New York • San Francisco • San Diego • New Haven, Conn.
Waterville, Maine • London • Munich

THOMSON
GALE

For more information, contact
Blackbirch Press
27500 Drake Rd.
Farmington Hills, MI 48331-3535
Or you can visit our Internet site at http://www.gale.com

Cover, upper left, Steve Zmina, upper right, © The Corcoran Gallery of Art/CORBIS, lower left and right, © Hulton Archive by Getty Images, lower middle, North Wind Picture Archives; © Bettmann/CORBIS, 10, 11, 14-15, 17, 25, 26-27, 32; © Brooklyn Museum of Art/CORBIS, 33; © The Corcoran Gallery of Art/CORBIS, 19; © CORBIS, 20, 34, 36, 37, 41, 42; © Peter M. Wilson/CORBIS, 40; © Galen Rowell/CORBIS, 38; © Hulton Archive by Getty Images, 22, 23, 30, 31; Library of Congress, 28; National Portrait Gallery, Smithsonian, 39, 43; North Wind Picture Archives, 39, 43; Steve Zmina, 21, 29.

LIBRARY OF CONGRESS CATALOGING-IN-PUBLICATION DATA

Bardhan-Quallen, Sudipta.
The Mexican-American War / by Sudipta Bardhan-Quallen.
p. cm. — (People at the center of)
Includes bibliographical references and index.
Audience: Grades 4–6.
ISBN 1-56711-927-1 (hardcover : alk. paper)
1. Mexican War, 1846–1848—Juvenile literature. 2. Mexican War, 1846–1848—Biography—Juvenile literature. I. Title. II. Series.
E404.B35 2005
973.6'2—dc22
2004013973

Printed in the United States of America

Contents

THE MEXICAN-AMERICAN WAR

In 1845, John L. O'Sullivan, editor of the *United States Magazine and Democratic Review*, wrote: "The American claim is by the right of our manifest destiny to overspread and to possess the whole of the continent which Providence has given us."[1] The term Sullivan coined, *manifest destiny*, described a popular political philosophy in the United States in the 1800s—that the United States could and should expand until its territory stretched from sea to shining sea. The problem, however, was that Mexico controlled a great amount of the western territory that lay adjacent to the United States. In fact, in the early 1800s, the borders of Mexico included present-day Texas, New Mexico, Colorado, Wyoming, Arizona, Utah, Nevada, and California.

While the 1800s marked a time of expansion for the United States, this same period was one of instability in Mexico. At the beginning of the nineteenth century, Mexico was a part of the empire of Spain. In 1810, a war for independence from Spain began. After eleven years of fighting, Mexicans gained their independence and established their own country. The subsequent years, however, were filled with internal power struggles and political strife over how to create a new and functional government. This instability in the government in part led to the Texas War for Independence in 1835. Texas, which had been a part of Mexico, had been populated by many Americans in the preceding years. Unhappy with Mexican rule, these American Texans fought against Mexico to create their own republic.

After Texas gained independence, there was a great deal of American support for the annexation of Texas by the United States. Mexicans, however, were not at all enthusiastic about American expansion. In fact, they were even split over Texas. Some Mexicans accepted Texan independence but argued over the southern border of the new republic (Texas claimed its border was the Rio Grande, whereas Mexico

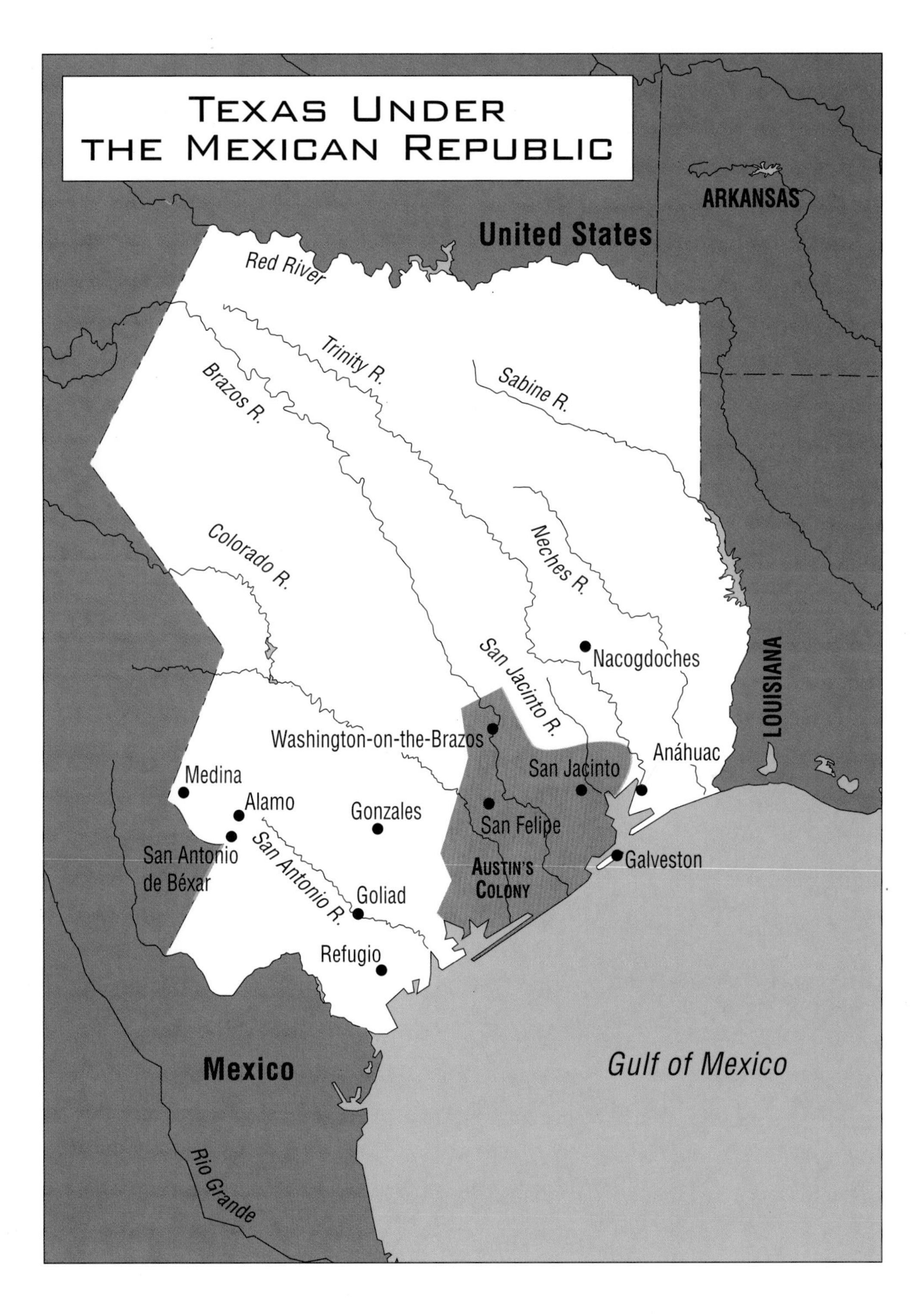
TEXAS UNDER THE MEXICAN REPUBLIC
United States
ARKANSAS
Red River
Trinity R.
Sabine R.
Brazos R.
Colorado R.
Neches R.
San Jacinto R.
Nacogdoches
LOUISIANA
Washington-on-the-Brazos
Anáhuac
San Jacinto
Medina
Alamo
Gonzales
San Felipe
San Antonio de Béxar
San Antonio R.
Galveston
Austin's Colony
Goliad
Refugio
Mexico
Gulf of Mexico
Rio Grande

contended it was the Nueces River). Many other Mexicans felt that Texas should be reannexed by Mexico. When outgoing American president John Tyler had Congress annex Texas through a joint resolution, the Mexican government immediately cut diplomatic ties with the United States, enraged that the Americans would lay claim to Mexican territory.

Still, Mexican president José Joaquín Herrera's administration seemed willing to negotiate with the United States over Texas. Newly elected president James Polk sent a representative, John Slidell, to discuss a way to purchase territory from Mexico in order to avoid further difficulties in the relations between the two nations over Tyler's joint resolution. Polk's intention, however, was to buy not only Texas but the Mexican territories of New Mexico and California as well.

Mexicans were outraged by Polk's proposal. Though some were prepared to let Texas go, the rest of Polk's plan proved to be too bitter a pill to swallow. Slidell was sent back to the United States without ever meeting with Mexican leaders.

The United States then mounted a three-pronged military plan to acquire the territories that Mexico refused to sell. General Zachary Taylor was sent to the disputed border of Texas, General Stephen Kearny was sent to New Mexico, and the U.S. Navy was sent into the Gulf of Mexico to establish a blockade of Mexican ports. Polk hoped that the presence of the American military would pressure Mexico into negotiating a sale of the desired lands. If Mexico would not negotiate, the United States could conquer the lands by force.

Fighting broke out on April 25, 1846, when Mexican forces attacked a group of American soldiers. Each side considered the battle to have been fought on its own soil. This attack helped Polk convince Congress to officially declare war on Mexico.

The Americans proceeded to win every major battle of the Mexican-American War, even though the Mexican forces were often greater in number. Many historians believe that the United States won the war because the American officers were better trained and the American soldiers had better weapons and supplies. Mexican soldiers were often forced to march in harsh conditions without proper food, water, or supplies and were even forced to use old and often unusable weapons. For example, at the Battle of Palo Alto, General Mariano Arista's men tried to fire upon American troops but their artillery shells failed to explode.

Another factor that hurt Mexico's efforts in the war was the political upheaval the country was still undergoing. For example, between 1833 and 1855, Mexico had thirty-six presidents. Some people, like Antonio López de Santa Anna and Herrera, served multiple terms as president, although their terms were interrupted by other political factions and leaders. Because of the infighting within the Mexican ranks,

James K. Polk's proposal to buy the California and New Mexico territories as well as Texas outraged the Mexican people.

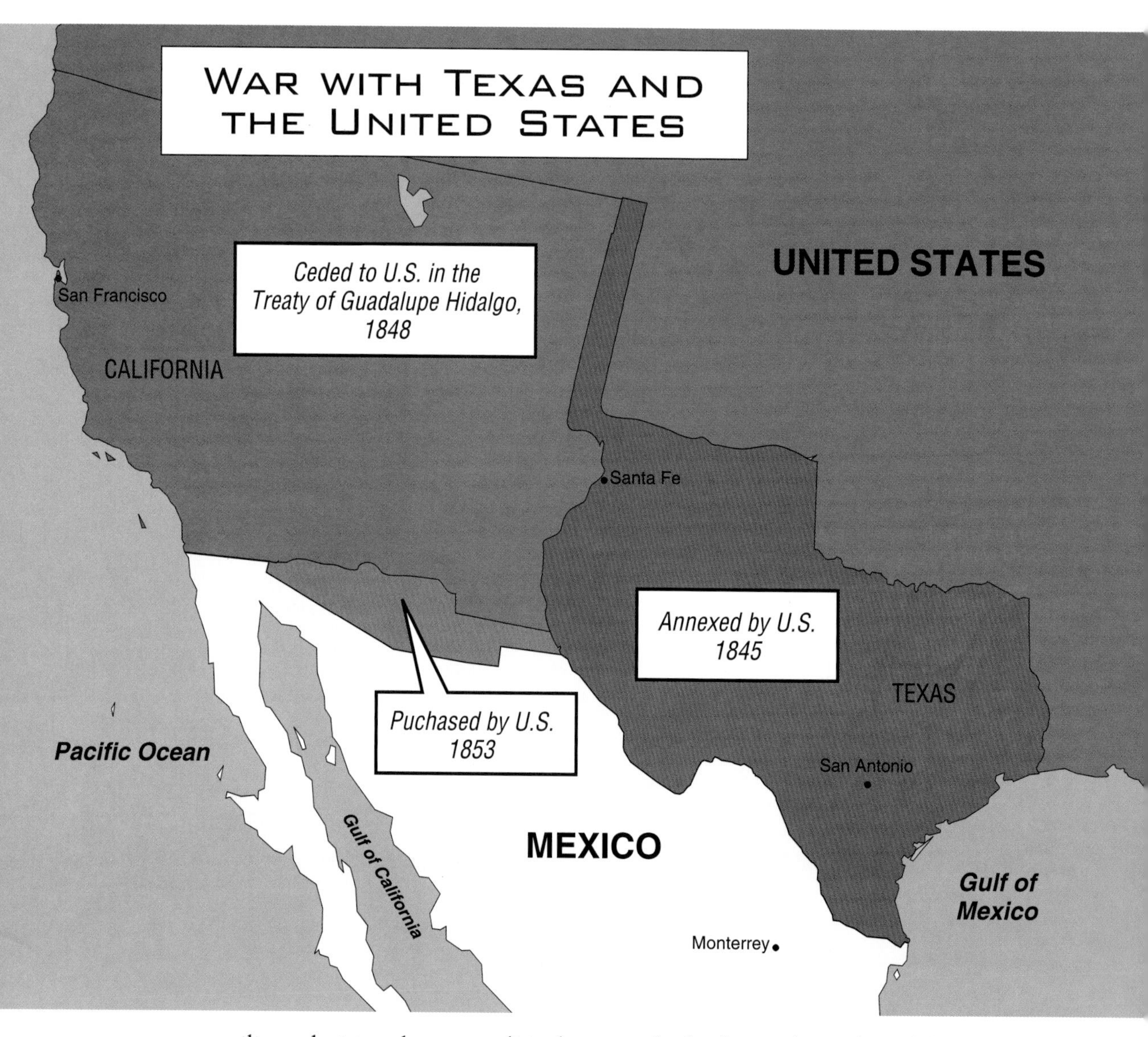

many military decisions became political issues, which ultimately weakened the Mexican armies.

As a result of the Mexican-American War, Mexico's territory was cut almost in half, whereas the United States gained 529,000 square miles of valuable land. The acquisition, however, led to a bitter quarrel between the North and the South over the expansion of slavery. Abolitionists wanted to ban slavery from all territory acquired from Mexico, whereas proponents of slavery disagreed. Many abolitionists even felt it would be better not to expand the United States at all if that expansion created more slave territory. Eventually, this quarrel over slavery resulted in the American Civil War.

In fact, many historians consider the Mexican-American War to have been a practice run for the Civil War. Many of the officers—including Robert E. Lee, Ulysses S. Grant, Thomas "Stonewall" Jackson, and dozens of others—who played pivotal roles in the Civil War actually received their battle training during the Mexican-American War. Even many of the tactics that proved successful during the Mexican-American War were reused during the Civil War—most notably, perhaps, was the Union navy's blockade of Confederate ports.

SAM HOUSTON

LEADER WHO HELPED WIN TEXAS INDEPENDENCE

Sam Houston was born in Virginia on March 2, 1793. He received very little formal schooling before his father died when Sam was thirteen years old. Afterward, his mother moved the family to Tennessee, where Houston lived for three years with the Cherokee Indians.

Houston served briefly in the military and then became a lawyer. Later, he served in Congress and, in 1827, was elected governor of Tennessee. Personal problems drove him from Tennessee, and in 1832, Houston headed to the Mexican territory of Texas.

Houston quickly became involved in Texas politics, supporting the American Texans in their bid for independence. In 1836, he supported the decision to declare independence from Mexico and was soon elected commander in chief of the armies of Texas.

After the Battle of San Jacinto, captured Mexican general Antonio López de Santa Anna is brought before Sam Houston.

After the revolutionary forces suffered initial defeats, Houston retreated with his troops as Mexican general Antonio López de Santa Anna swept across Texas. Houston finally faced Santa Anna on April 21, 1836, in the Battle of San Jacinto. He won a decisive victory and captured Santa Anna.

Texas won its independence at San Jacinto, and Houston was elected the first president of the Republic of Texas. He wanted the United States to annex Texas at that time, but the two governments could not come to an agreement. Still, Houston's efforts to gain independence for Texas was the first step toward the eventual annexation of Texas by the United States, and therefore the Mexican-American War.

Houston was active in Texas politics for the rest of his life. He served two terms as president, as a member of the Texas House of Representatives, and, after Texas joined the United States, as a U.S. Senator and as governor of Texas.

In 1862, retired from politics, Houston moved his family to Huntsville, Texas. After being ill with pneumonia for several weeks, he died on July 26, 1863.

Sam Houston helped Texas win independence. He served as the first president of the Republic of Texas, and later as governor of the state of Texas.

Antonio López de Santa Anna

Supreme commander of all Mexican forces

Antonio López de Santa Anna was born in Veracruz on February 21, 1794. At sixteen, he began his military career; by 1828, he was the highest-ranking general in Mexico.

In 1833, Santa Anna was elected president of Mexico. During the Texas War for Independence, he brutally defeated Texan revolutionaries at initial battles at the Alamo and Goliad. However, he was then defeated and captured at the Battle of San Jacinto in 1836. Mexico renounced him as president, and Santa Anna was exiled to the United States until 1837.

In the years between 1837 and the Mexican-American War, Santa Anna became president again and was exiled again. Upon the American declaration of war on Mexico in 1846, Santa Anna vigorously opposed any concessions to the United States. He returned to Mexico, became supreme commander of the Mexican forces, and prepared for battle.

At the Battle of Buena Vista on February 22, 1847, Santa Anna's forces greatly outnumbered Zachary Taylor's troop—fifteen thousand Mexicans versus five thousand Americans. Unfortunately for Santa Anna, his men had been pushed too hard. By the time the armies met, the Mexicans were tired, hungry, and thirsty. They battled the Americans for two days, but then became too exhausted to continue fighting. Santa Anna withdrew his men from the field, ending the battle and handing the victory to Taylor.

Santa Anna hurried southward toward Mexico City to defend the capital against Winfield Scott's forces. He quickly took advantage of political upheaval in the capital to assume the presidency again. His army faced Scott's at Cerro Gordo on April 18. Once again, Santa Anna commanded the larger force, but the Mexicans were again defeated. Santa Anna had to escape on foot to prevent being captured.

Santa Anna faced Scott in battle one final time on September 13 as they fought for Mexico City. By late that evening, an American victory was imminent, and Santa Anna resigned his presidency and fled to avoid being captured. His leadership during the war was marked by missed opportunities and self-serving political maneuvering, which contributed to his country's defeat. On September 14, the acting president, Manuel de la Peña y Peña, surrendered the city. Soon after, negotiations to end the war began.

General Antonio López de Santa Anna enjoyed victories and suffered many defeats in his military career.

After the Mexican-American War ended, Santa Anna went back and forth between exile and retaking the presidency. Eventually, even his allies had had enough of him, and he was exiled once more in 1855. He did not return to Mexico until 1874, under a general amnesty. He died in relative obscurity on June 21, 1876.

Santa Anna leads his men at the Battle of Buena Vista in 1847. He had to withdraw his exhausted troops.

JOHN TYLER

U.S. PRESIDENT WHO GRANTED TEXAS STATEHOOD

John Tyler was born on March 29, 1790, in Virginia. He graduated from the College of William and Mary at the age of seventeen. Afterward, he practiced law and then entered politics. Tyler served in the House of Representatives, as the governor of Virginia, and as a U.S. Senator before being elected vice president in 1840.

When President William Henry Harrison died in April 1841, just weeks after his inauguration, Tyler became president. He faced opposition from almost everyone, including his own cabinet, because he was the first vice president to be elevated to the presidency. Some people continued to call him "acting president" well into his term.

Tyler faced hostility when he ran for reelection in 1844. He proposed to annex Texas as a way to gather support for his candidacy. Unfortunately for Tyler, his opponent, James Polk, endorsed Texas statehood as well. This weakened Tyler's strategy for the election, and he eventually withdrew from the race. Polk won after he defeated the only other remaining candidate, Henry Clay.

One of Tyler's last acts as president, which occurred just three days before Polk was inaugurated, was to annex Texas into the United States. Tyler did not have time to finalize a treaty with the Republic of Texas in his last few days in office, so he opted instead to propose a joint resolution, which was passed by Congress. Tyler signed the joint resolution that granted Texas statehood on March 1, 1845. Mexico, however, opposed this move and considered the annexation of Texas to be illegal. In effect, Tyler's move created the grounds for the Mexican-American War.

After his term in office, Tyler returned to Virginia. During the Civil War, he was a supporter of Southern secession. He was even elected to the House of Representatives of the Confederate Congress, but he died on January 18, 1862, before the Congress assembled.

President John Tyler annexed Texas to the United States in 1845. Mexico believed he had no right to do so.

JAMES K. POLK

U.S. PRESIDENT DURING THE MEXICAN-AMERICAN WAR

James Knox Polk was born on November 2, 1795, in North Carolina. He graduated from the University of North Carolina in 1818, and then practiced law until he entered politics. He served in the Tennessee legislature, in the House of Representatives, and as governor of Tennessee. In 1844, he ran successfully for president of the United States, campaigning on the idea that the country should expand westward.

Before Polk was sworn in, outgoing president John Tyler had Congress pass a joint resolution to annex Texas. This action created a strong probability of war with Mexico, as many Mexicans felt that Texas still was Mexican territory. Initially, Polk attempted to negotiate with Mexico by sending John Slidell to offer the Mexican government $30 million for the lands. When Slidell tried to purchase the lands, however, many Mexican leaders were offended. As a result, Slidell's diplomatic mission failed.

Zachary Taylor's army takes up position at the Rio Grande, an act that provoked war with Mexico.

Polk then sent Zachary Taylor's army to Texas to defend the area from Mexican invasion. Taylor was ordered to take up position at the mouth of the Rio Grande, the boundary that the Republic of Texas claimed. The adjacent Mexican state of Tamaulipas, however, insisted that the Texas border was actually farther north, at the Nueces River.

Americans who opposed the annexation of Texas claimed that Polk sent Taylor to the Rio Grande in the hopes that the Mexicans would attack, thus provoking a war. Sure enough, on April 25, 1846, a party led by Captain Seth Thornton was attacked by Mexican forces who considered Thornton to be invading Mexican soil. Polk used this event to urge Congress into taking action and forced a declaration of war on Mexico on May 13. This officially began the Mexican-American War.

In the ensuing months, American forces won battle after battle. By September 14, 1847, even Mexico City was under American control. Polk then sent diplomat Nicholas Trist to negotiate a peace with Mexico. The war officially ended on February 2, 1848.

Polk had promised early on that he would only serve one term as president. He remained true to his word, and he was succeeded by Taylor. Polk was exhausted by the burdens of the presidency and only lived three months after leaving office. He died at his estate in Nashville on June 15, 1849.

James K. Polk promoted westward expansion. He strongly supported the annexation of Texas.

José Joaquín Herrera

Mexican President Who Was Unable to Avoid the Mexican-American War

José Joaquín Herrera was born in Jalapa, Mexico, in 1792. At seventeen, he was promoted to the rank of captain; seven years later, he was a brigadier general. entered military service and proceeded to have a successful military career. By 1814, he was promoted to the rank of captain; seven years later he was a brigadier general.

In 1844, Herrera was appointed president of Mexico after Antonio López de Santa Anna resigned, but factions within Mexico immediately began planning to overthrow him. His actions during the annexation of Texas by the United States gave Herrera's opponents the opportunity they needed to oust him from office.

John Slidell went to Mexico to negotiate the surrender of Texas with José Joaquín Herrera.

Herrera was the first Mexican president willing to entertain the notion that Texas was lost to the United States forever. He attempted to prevent a war between the United States and Mexico by resolving the issue of the ownership of Texas. Herrera requested that President James Polk send a representative to Mexico to discuss terms under which Texas could be surrendered to the United States.

Polk, however, through his representative John Slidell, sent a list of demands that were impossible for Herrera to agree to. Most Mexicans chafed at the loss of Texas, yet Slidell attempted to purchase even more territory on behalf of the United States.

Herrera's opponents roused the Mexican public against any negotiations with Slidell to give up more Mexican lands. As a result, Herrera became increasingly unpopular. The leader of the opposition, Mariano Paredes y Arrillaga, even demanded an attack on the United States. Herrera attempted to save his administration by refusing to meet with Slidell when he arrived in Mexico in

José Joaquín Herrera served as president of Mexico during the Mexican-American War. Herrera favored the annexation of Texas.

December 1845, but by then, it was too late. Paredes led a rebellion against Herrera on December 14. By January 2, 1846, Herrera had been ousted from office, and Paredes had assumed the presidency.

After the Mexican-American War ended with the Treaty of Guadalupe Hidalgo, Herrera again served briefly as president. Afterward, Herrera retired to Tacubaya, where he died on February 10, 1854.

As its president, Mariano Paredes y Arrillaga pushed Mexico into war with the United States.

Mariano Paredes y Arrillaga

Mexican President who officially declared war on the United States

Mariano Paredes y Arrillaga was born in Mexico City on January 7, 1797. In 1812, he joined the army in the Regimiento de Infantería de Mexico, and by 1832, he was a brigadier general.

Paredes entered politics in 1835, first as a supporter of Antonio López de Santa Anna. Over the years, he switched allegiances a number of times. As early as 1841, Paredes was criticizing the government of Mexico for not having tried to recover Texas. He felt strongly that Texas should remain a part of Mexico.

When President José Joaquín Herrera indicated a willingness to negotiate with the United States over Texas, Paredes led a rebellion against him on December 14, 1845. As a result of the rebellion, Paredes was named interim president of Mexico in early January 1846. The Mexican Congress formally elected him president on June 20, 1846.

In March 1846, Zachary Taylor took up position on the Texas-Mexico border, an area the Americans considered to be in dispute. Paredes did not acknowledge any disputed boundary—he considered the entire area to be Mexican territory. On April 4, Paredes ordered the Mexican army to attack Taylor, but the local commander delayed in following the order. In response, Paredes issued a formal declaration of war on the United States on April 23. Paredes's actions officially began the Mexican-American War for Mexico. Within days, Mexican troops engaged American soldiers for the first time.

Mexican soldiers battle Zachary Taylor's army at Monterrey, an important fortress in Mexico.

Though Paredes was heavily involved in the commencement of the war, by August 1846, a rebellion removed him from power. At first, he was imprisoned, and then exiled to Paris, France, in October 1846.

After the end of the war, Paredes returned to Mexico and attempted to stage another rebellion against the government. He was unsuccessful and was exiled once again. He finally returned to Mexico under a general amnesty in April 1849, but died in poverty in Mexico City five months later.

ZACHARY TAYLOR

AMERICAN GENERAL

Zachary Taylor was born on November 24, 1784, in Virginia to a wealthy family of planters. He was a poor student; in fact, throughout his life, his grammar, spelling, and handwriting were crude and rough.

Taylor received his first military commission in 1808 and was assigned to one frontier post after another. An able soldier, he gained national fame at the start of the Mexican-American War.

In March 1846, President James Polk ordered him to the disputed Texas-Mexico border. Soon after he arrived, his men were attacked by Mexican forces on April 25. When Taylor heard of the attack, he sent a message to Polk to inform him that hostilities had begun.

Even before Congress officially declared war, Taylor engaged Mexican forces led by Mariano Arista in the Battle of Palo Alto on May 8. Taylor won the battle, forcing Arista to retreat south. The next day, Taylor again engaged Arista's army at the Battle of Resaca de la Palma. Once more, the Mexicans were defeated, with few American casualties.

Following his victory at Resaca de la Palma, Taylor spent two months training reinforcements before marching toward the city of Monterrey in the state of Nuevo León, Mexico. Pedro de Ampudia unsuccessfully attempted to defend Monterrey. After a four-day siege, Ampudia approached Taylor to negotiate a truce. On September 28, it was agreed that the Mexican forces would surrender and then be allowed to withdraw from the city in eight weeks. Taylor had conquered another important city as he made his way south toward central Mexico.

With another victory at the Battle of Buena Vista in February 1847, Taylor became an American hero. He had consistently defeated much larger Mexican forces, prevented his troops from experiencing many casualties, and had fought alongside his men in hand-to-hand combat time and again. After the end of the war, Taylor's popularity propelled him into the White House.

As president, Taylor was a strong nationalist and vigorously opposed Southern secession. Taylor was not able to influence the issue of secession too much, however—he only served sixteen months in office. He contracted a stomach ailment and died on June 9, 1850.

General Zachary Taylor is shown on the Mexican battlefield. Taylor's army won the Battle of Palo Alto.

Troops clash at the Battle of Palo Alto, the first major battle of the war with Mexico.

MARIANO ARISTA

MEXICAN GENERAL

Mariano Arista was born on July 26, 1802, in San Luis Potosí, Mexico. When he was fifteen years old, he joined the army as a cadet in the Puebla regiment. He quickly rose to the rank of brigadier general and later served with Antonio López de Santa Anna during the failed attempt to subdue the Texas War for Independence.

At the start of the Mexican-American War, Arista was given the command of the Mexican Army of the North. He was dispatched to oust Taylor's American forces from the Texas-Mexico border. Instead, Arista's army suffered defeat after defeat at Taylor's hands, first at the Battle of Palo Alto and later at the Battle of Resaca de la Palma, even though Arista commanded the larger force. One reason for his failure was that because his political views were in disagreement with those of his staff, he faced opposition from within his own ranks at every turn.

Mariano Arista commanded Mexican forces at Resaca de la Palma, site of the second battle of the Mexican-American War.

Arista was forced to retreat farther and farther south. After losing the Battle of Resaca de la Palma, Arista was removed from command by the Mexican government. For the rest of the war, he saw little combat.

Later, Arista demanded a court martial to determine whether he was to blame for the defeats at Palo Alto and Resaca de la Palma. He was absolved of all guilt in those proceedings. His story, however, represented a major problem faced by Mexico during the war—that military decisions became so politicized that leaders like Arista could not win battles. After the war ended, Arista became secretary of war in June 1848 and then was declared constitutional president by the Mexican Congress in January 1851.

Arista tried to stabilize his country during his presidency, but faced great opposition from political rivals. Eventually, his opponents revolted against him, and he was forced to resign from the presidency and go into exile in January 1853.

Arista died near Lisbon, Portugal, on August 7, 1855. After his death, he was honored in Mexico as a hero, and his remains were returned to his homeland for burial.

Mariano Arista led the Mexican army against Zachary Taylor's troops. He lost the Battles of Palo Alto and Resaca de la Palma.

WINFIELD SCOTT

COMMANDING GENERAL OF THE UNITED STATES ARMY

Winfield Scott was born on June 13, 1786, near Petersburg, Virginia. Both of Scott's parents died when he was young, and Scott studied at the College of William and Mary for a short time after their deaths. Eventually, he joined the army in 1808, and he became a hero of the War of 1812 and the Black Hawk War.

In 1841, Scott was named commanding general of the U.S. Army. When the Mexican-American War broke out, Scott led an army into Mexico. He planned a daring attack on the Mexican city of Veracruz by transporting his troops over the sea. With a force of twelve thousand men, Scott landed about three miles south of Veracruz on March 9, 1847, and proceeded to surround the city. After a twenty-day siege, the city fell to Scott; the American forces had sustained only a handful of casualties.

General Winfield Scott's soldiers enter Mexico City in 1847. Scott boldly moved his troops by sea.

Scott continued inland with a force of eighty-five hundred troops. On April 18, 1847, he encountered Antonio López de Santa Anna at the Battle of Cerro Gordo. Though Santa Anna's force was larger, Scott managed to surround the Mexican troops and win the victory.

Scott pressed forward, on to Mexico City, winning the battles of Molino del Roy on September 8 and Chapultepec on September 13 along the way. Finally, he took Mexico City on September 14 after a two-day battle. During his five-month campaign, Scott had won every battle decisively. His military leadership allowed the Americans to win the Mexican-American War despite having fewer troops and fighting on foreign soil.

After the end of the Mexican-American War, Scott retained his position as commanding general of the Army for many years. At the outbreak of the Civil War, Scott was considered by many to be too old at age seventy-five to command the Union Army. He retired on November 1, 1861, but his suggested strategy of a naval blockade of Confederate ports was one of the keys to the Union's victory.

Scott died on May 29, 1866. Though he never attended the U.S. military academy at West Point, he is buried there.

Winfield Scott led the American forces during the Mexican-American War. Scott's campaigns were very successful.

JOHN CHARLES FRÉMONT

ENCOURAGED CALIFORNIA SETTLERS TO REVOLT AGAINST MEXICO

John Charles Frémont was born in Savannah, Georgia, on January 21, 1813. He attended Charleston College but was expelled before completing a degree. Later, he worked as a civil engineer for the army.

In 1845, Frémont, by then a major, was on a military expedition in California, which was still officially a part of Mexico. There, he encouraged American settlers to revolt against Mexico, which was the first step in establishing an independent California republic. On June 14, 1846, Frémont led the Bear Flag Revolt at Sonoma and forced Mexican colonel Mariano Vallejo to surrender. Frémont's victory was completely bloodless and gave the United States a great military advantage over Mexico in the midst of the Mexican-American War.

During the Bear Flag Revolt in Sonoma, John Frémont raises the flag of the new California Republic.

Frémont sent word to General Stephen Kearny that California was now in the hands of American forces. When Kearny finally made it to California, Frémont clashed with him over the command. Commodore Robert Stockton sided with Frémont and subsequently named Frémont military governor. In that capacity, Frémont oversaw Mexico's actions on January 13, 1847, to relinquish California to the United States.

Kearny eventually received orders from Washington to assume command of California. Still angry at Frémont, Kearny had him court martialed for insubordination on August 22, 1847. Frémont was found guilty of mutiny and disobedience of the lawful command of a superior officer. The court's recommendation was that Frémont be forced to resign from the military, though it also recommended that

Frémont's Bear Flag Revolt led to the admission of California to the Union in 1850.

President James Polk show clemency toward Frémont.

Polk removed the conviction for mutiny but let the rest of the verdict stand, and he removed the penalty. Frémont, however, found the verdict so offensive that he resigned anyway.

Later in life, Frémont served in the Senate and even unsuccessfully ran for president in 1856. President Abraham Lincoln placed him in command of the western military district from May 1861 to December 1861. Frémont also served as governor of the Arizona Territory from 1878 to 1881. After retirement, Frémont died in New York City on July 13, 1890.

In 1846 Stephen Watts Kearny captured the New Mexico Territory from Mexico without firing a single shot.

Stephen Watts Kearny

American General and Commander of the Army of the West

Stephen Watts Kearny was born in New Jersey on August 30, 1794. He studied at Columbia College until he joined the army during the War of 1812. His courageous service during this war helped to launch a career in the military.

By 1846, he was the commander of the Army of the West. When the Mexican-American War broke out, President James Polk ordered Kearny into Santa Fe. Kearny proceeded to take control of New Mexico without firing a single shot. Throughout the war, Kearny's diplomacy and military competence gained him decisive victories, which helped the United States defeat Mexico.

From Santa Fe, Kearny headed toward Arizona and California. Along the way, Kearny encountered a scout who carried a message from Major John Frémont, saying that American settlers had taken California in the Bear Flag Revolt. Kearny headed to San Diego with a small contingent of one hundred men.

Frémont, however, had overstated his success, and Kearny was unprepared when he was ambushed by armed Californios (Mexican inhabitants of California) in the Battle of San Pasqual. The Californios wanted to bar more American soldiers from invading their homeland. Kearny's poorly supplied men were badly outnumbered. Kearny was forced to wait for reinforcements from Robert Stockton and Frémont.

The reinforcements were delayed, but when they finally arrived, the Californios were defeated. Kearny continued his march to San Diego. Kearny's forces, combined with Stockton's, were able to conquer San Gabriel and Los Angeles in January 1847.

Kearny was the ranking officer, and he attempted to take command of California. Stockton, however, resisted Kearny's command. In fact, when the last Mexican forces in the region surrendered to Frémont, Stockton took the opportunity to name Frémont the military governor. Frémont refused to acknowledge Kearny's authority.

Kearny was angered by the actions of Stockton and Frémont. He protested to Washington and soon received confirmation of his command. Kearny then had Frémont arrested and became the official and uncontested military governor.

Kearny remained the military governor of California through August 1847. Later, as the Americans won battles in and occupied Mexico, he served as governor of Veracruz, Mexico, and then of Mexico City. He contracted a tropical disease in Veracruz, which caused his death on October 31, 1848.

As a congressman, Abraham Lincoln was one of the few politicians opposed to the Mexican-American War.

ABRAHAM LINCOLN

CONGRESSMAN WHO QUESTIONED THE REASONS FOR THE MEXICAN-AMERICAN WAR

Abraham Lincoln was born in a log cabin in Kentucky on February 12, 1809. In 1816, his parents moved the Lincoln family from Kentucky to Indiana, partly because slavery was forbidden in Indiana. Lincoln learned to disapprove of slavery from his family's strong views on the subject.

Lincoln attended less than a year of school; nonetheless, he could read, write, and do arithmetic. Over the years, he worked at a number of jobs, including rail-splitter, postmaster, surveyor, and storekeeper. Eventually, he entered politics and was elected to the Illinois legislature in 1834.

Abraham Lincoln wipes his brow while splitting rails, one of his many jobs.

By 1847, Lincoln had been elected to the House of Representatives. By then, Congress had already declared war with Mexico after President James Polk stated, "Mexico has passed the boundary of the United States, has invaded our territory and shed American blood upon America's soil."[2]

Lincoln was one of the few people in Congress to question whether American soil had been invaded and whether the spot upon which blood was shed was U.S. territory. On December 22, 1847, Lincoln introduced the "spot resolutions," which demanded more information from Polk about the facts that led up to the declaration of war.

Though Congress did not act on the spot resolutions, Lincoln was criticized for his opposition to the war. He was branded a traitor, and one Illinois newspaper nicknamed him "spotty Lincoln." Lincoln became very unpopular in his district and failed to win reelection in 1849. He withdrew from politics for approximately five years.

In the long run, though, Lincoln's stance against the Mexican-American War did not hurt his political career. In 1860, Lincoln was elected president, and he served through the Civil War. He issued the Emancipation Proclamation, which freed slaves in Confederate states. After the Union won the Civil War, Lincoln was trying to help the nation heal when he was shot by John Wilkes Booth on April 14, 1865. Lincoln died the next day.

HENRY DAVID THOREAU

PHILOSOPHER AND ABOLITIONIST WHO PROTESTED THE MEXICAN-AMERICAN WAR

Henry David Thoreau was born on July 12, 1817, in Concord, Massachusetts. He graduated from Harvard University in 1837. In 1841, Thoreau began working in the house of writer and philosopher Ralph Waldo Emerson as a handyman. There, he studied and wrote about philosophy, nature, and even political causes.

Of all the essays that Thoreau wrote, one of the most famous was titled "Civil Disobedience," which discussed an event that occurred in 1846. Thoreau was staying at Walden Pond in order to read, write, and experience nature. On July 23, he went into Concord to pick up a shoe at the cobblers' shop. The tax collector, Sam Staples, asked Thoreau to pay his poll tax. Thoreau refused, since he objected to the government's use of tax money to support the Mexican-American War. Thoreau believed that if the United States won territory from Mexico, slavery would be allowed in the new lands. As a staunch abolitionist, he opposed the war heartily.

Henry David Thoreau lived and worked near Walden Pond, writing his famous essays.

Staples arrested Thoreau for failing to pay his taxes, and Thoreau spent the night in jail. The next morning, he was released after someone paid the taxes on his behalf. This infuriated Thoreau—he was willing to spend a lot more time in jail to protest what he considered an immoral use of tax money.

In "Civil Disobedience," Thoreau encouraged others to take the same stand as he did when government acted against a person's beliefs. He wrote: "Unjust laws exist; shall we be content to obey them, or shall we endeavor to amend them, and obey them until we have succeeded, or shall we transgress them at once?"[3]

Thoreau's gesture did not stop the Mexican-American War, but it represented the sentiments of many Americans who felt the war was being fought for the wrong reasons. In addition, Thoreau's failure did not discourage him from fighting against slavery. He worked with the Underground Railroad to help runaway slaves. Thoreau died on May 6, 1862, of tuberculosis, and many of his works were published posthumously.

Thoreau was a naturalist and philosopher who believed the Mexican-American War was immoral.

A LOS DEFENSORES DE LA PATRIA
1846 1847

Los Niños Héroes

Mexican youths who sacrificed themselves for their country

Beginning in 1833, Chapultepec Castle served as Mexico's military academy, where the sons of Mexico's finest families learned the art of war. In 1847, Chapultepec was home to fifty cadets, including Juan de la Barrera, Juan Escutia, Agustin Melgar, Fernando Montes de Oca, Vicente Suarez, and Francisco Márquez, the youngest of the group at thirteen years old.

On September 13, 1847, American forces led by General Winfield Scott began an attack on the castle. Beforehand, the school's director ordered the cadets to leave Chapultepec. They refused and chose instead to fight alongside the soldiers defending the school.

Unfortunately for the cadets, there were just over eight hundred Mexican defenders at Chapultepec that day. They faced a much larger American force, one that was determined to prevail over the Mexican resistance.

Within two hours of fighting, the Americans had overrun and taken Chapultepec Castle. Some of the cadets were captured and taken as prisoners of war. De la Barrera, Escutia, Melgar, de Oca, Suarez, and Márquez, however, were among the great number of Mexican dead. They had been bayoneted and shot where they stood. Escutia, who had been guarding the castle's flag, had wrapped it around himself and leaped from the castle walls to prevent the flag from falling into American hands.

American soldiers storm the fortress of Chapultepec Castle in Mexico City.

Because of their bravery, the six cadets who died at Chapultepec are honored each year in Mexico as "Los Niños Héroes" (the child heroes). In fact, they were considered by Mexicans to be the embodiment of their countrymen's willingness to fight for their homeland. A number of monuments to them can be found throughout Mexico, and the cadets were even honored on Mexican currency.

This monument in Chapultepec Park to the child heroes is one of many found in Mexico.

Nicholas Philip Trist

Diplomat who negotiated the end of the Mexican-American War

Nicholas Philip Trist was born on June 2, 1800, in Virginia. He graduated from the College of Orleans in 1817, then studied law with Thomas Jefferson. He later worked for the State Department.

In 1847, Trist was sent to negotiate a treaty to end the Mexican-American War, with a draft of a treaty proposal to use as a guide. President James Polk had instructed Trist to claim the Rio Grande as the southwestern boundary of Texas. The Mexicans, however, insisted that the boundary be the Nueces River. Initially, Trist negotiated a preliminary agreement that granted many of the American demands but held the border at the Nueces River.

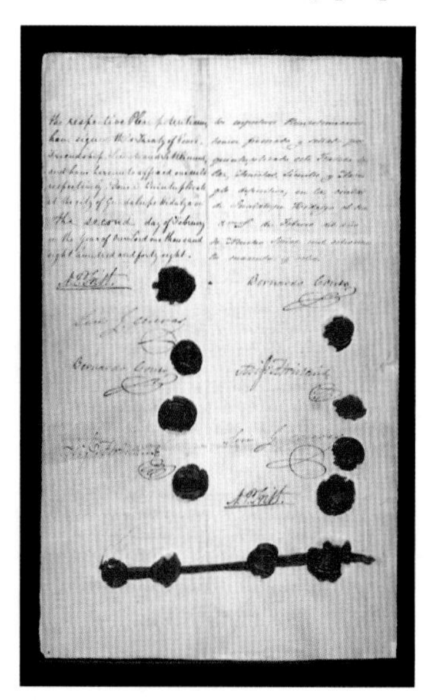

The signed Treaty of Guadalupe Hidalgo included the signature of Nicholas Philip Trist.

Polk was enraged by Trist's concessions and recalled Trist on October 8, 1847. Trist, however, was not willing to give up what he viewed as the only opportunity for peace. He continued to negotiate with the Mexican representatives, although he was no longer an official diplomat.

In the end, it was Trist's tireless efforts that brought about the official end of the war. He persuaded the Mexicans to cede all of California from San Diego northward, New Mexico, and Texas at the Rio Grande border. In return, the United States would pay Mexico $15 million. In fact, Trist's final draft of the Treaty of Guadalupe Hidalgo, signed on February 2, 1848, covered all of Polk's original terms.

Polk was upset that Trist had ignored a presidential order to withdraw from negotiations, but because of rising antiwar sentiment in the United States, he sent the treaty to be ratified by Congress. By July 4, 1848, all terms were agreed upon by both countries, and the Mexican-American War had come to an end.

Trist negotiated the Treaty of Guadalupe Hidalgo, bringing an end to the war with Mexico.

Unfortunately for Trist, his political career ended with the Treaty of Guadalupe Hidalgo. Polk even refused to pay Trist his salary and reimbursement for expenses from the mission; Trist did not receive those payments until 1871. Trist went on to live in relative obscurity until his death in Virginia on February 11, 1874.

CHRONOLOGY

March 2, 1836	Texas declares independence from Mexico.
April 21, 1836	Texans win the Battle of San Jacinto and form a republic.
February 28, 1845	U.S. Congress votes to annex Texas.
March 1, 1845	President Tyler signs the joint resolution to grant Texas statehood.
January 1, 1846	President Polk orders Taylor to the disputed Texas border.
April 25, 1846	Mexican forces fire on an American party led by Seth Thornton, which constitutes the first shots of the war.
May 8, 1846	Taylor defeats Arista in the Battle of Palo Alto.
May 9, 1846	Taylor defeats Arista a second time in the Battle of Resaca de la Palma.
May 13, 1846	The United States declares war on Mexico.
June 14, 1846	Frémont declares California independent of Mexico in the Bear Flag Revolt.
August 1846	Kearny takes Santa Fe.
September 20–24, 1846	Taylor defeats Pedro de Ampudia at the Battle of Monterrey.
December 6, 1846	Kearny captures San Gabriel and Los Angeles, and fighting in California ends.
February 22–23, 1847	Taylor defeats Santa Anna at the Battle of Buena Vista despite being outnumbered.
March 9–29, 1847	Scott sieges Veracruz.
April 18, 1847	Scott defeats Santa Anna at the Battle of Cerro Gordo.

September 8, 1847	**Scott wins the Battle of Molino del Rey.**
September 13, 1847	**Scott wins the Battle of Chapultepec. Six young men, Los Niños Héroes, die defending Chapultepec Castle against Scott's forces.**
September 13–14, 1847	**Scott battles for and wins Mexico City. The city surrenders, and Scott raises the American flag at the national palace.**
December 22, 1847	**Lincoln introduces the "spot resolutions," demanding information from Polk about the facts that led up to the declaration of war.**
February 2, 1848	**Treaty of Guadalupe Hidalgo is signed, officially ending the war.**

For Further Information

Books

Richard Nelson Current, T. Harry Williams, and Frank Freidel, *A Survey of American History*. Vol. 1, New York: Knopf, 1983.

Philip R. Katcher, *The Mexican-American War, 1846–1848*. Oxford, Great Britain: Osprey, 1989.

Douglas V. Mead, *The Mexican War, 1846–1848*. Oxford, Great Britain: Osprey, 2002.

Don Nardo, *The Mexican-American War*. San Diego: Lucent, 1999.

Kim A. O'Connell, *The Mexican-American War*, Berkeley Heights, NJ: Enslow, 2003.

Web Sites

The U.S. Mexican War (1846–1848)
www.pbs.org/kera/usmexicanwar
This Web site accompanies the documentary *The U.S.-Mexican War (1846–1848)*. The site contains essays and commentaries by historians and other experts on different aspects of the Mexican-American War.

The U.S. Mexican War
www.dmwv.org/mexwar/mexwar1.htm
A comprehensive site that features articles, images, documents, and maps pertaining to the Mexican-American War.

Notes

1. Quoted in Richard Nelson Current, T. Harry Williams, and Frank Freidel, *A Survey of American History, Vol. 1*, New York: Knopf, 1983, p. 375.

2. Quoted in *PBS–The West*, "James K. Polk Message on War with Mexico, May 11, 1846." www.pbs.org/weta/thewest/resources/archives/two/mexdec.htm.

3. Henry David Thoreau, "Civil Disobedience," *Transcendentalists*. www.transcen dentalists.com.

About the Author

Sudipta Bardhan-Quallen holds a bachelor's degree and a master's degree, both in biology, from the California Institute of Technology. Her writing interests range from nonfiction for young adults to poetry for children. She lives in New Jersey with her husband and two daughters.

Index